Poseidon Oceanic Multipurpose System

Russia's Nuclear Strike Undersea Drone

Hugh Harkins

Copyright © 2019 Hugh Harkins

All rights reserved.

ISBN: 1-903630-85-1
ISBN-13: 978-1-903630-85-3

Poseidon Oceanic Multipurpose System

Russia's Nuclear Strike Undersea Drone

© Hugh Harkins 2019

Published by Centurion Publishing
United Kingdom

ISBN 10: 1-903630-83-5
ISBN 13: 978-1-903630-83-9

This volume first published in 2019

The Author is identified as the copyright holder of this work under sections 77 and 78 of the Copyright Designs and Patents Act 1988

Cover design © Centurion Publishing & KDP

Page layout, concept and design © Centurion Publishing

All rights reserved. No part of this publication may be reproduced, stored in a retrieval system, transmitted in any form, or by any means, electronic, mechanical or photocopied, recorded or otherwise, without the written permission of the publisher

The publisher and author would like to thank all organisations and services for their assistance and contributions in the preparation of this volume: Ministry of Defence of the Russian Federation; Press Service of the Kremlin, Government of the Russian Federation; JSC PO Sevmash; JSC Malachite SPB, Sea Bureau of Mechanical Engineering; Zvezdochka Shipyard JSC and TASS (News Agency)

Citation guide: Ministry of Defence of the Russian Federation (MODRF); Press Service of the Kremlin, Government of the Russian Federation (Kremlin Press Service); JSC PO Sevmash (PO Sevmash); JSC Malachite SPB, Sea Bureau of Mechanical Engineering (Malachite); Zvezdochka Shipyard JSC (STAR); TASS (News Agency) (TASS); Harkins, H. (2018) 'Russian/Soviet Submarine Launched Ballistic Missiles, Nuclear Deterrence/Counter Force Strike', Centurion Publishing (Harkins, 2018); Harkins, H. (2019) 'Russian Littoral Submarines & Submersibles – Piranha/Piranha-T/P-550/P-650E/Triton-I/II/Rus & Bester', Centurion Publishing (Harkins, 2019)

CONTENTS

	INTRODUCTION	vii
1	POSEIDON OCEANIC MULTIPURPOSE SYSTEM	1
2	GLOSSARY	22

INTRODUCTION

The purpose of this volume is to provide a short overview of the Poseidon Oceanic Multipurpose System, which remains, in 2019, shrouded in the highest levels of classification within the Russian Federation political and defence establishments. Poseidon is being developed as an element of the nuclear deterrent forces of the Russian Federation as that nation pushes to overcome perceived NATO alliance attempts to move from a position of nuclear parity to a position of nuclear superiority.

All graphic and photographic material has been furnished by the Ministry of Defence of the Russian Federation and various design bureau.

1

POSEIDON OCEANIC MULTIPURPOSE SYSTEM

The existence of the Poseidon (Посейдон) Oceanic Multipurpose System development was revealed by the Russian Federation President during a state of the nation address on 1 Match 2018 (the Poseidon name was allocated after this date). The Poseidon system is one of a number of new technology developments being pursued to ensure a viable multi-faceted strategic nuclear deterrent for the Russian Federation in the face of what that nation perceives as NATO (North Atlantic Treaty Organisation) attempts to tip the strategic balance in its favour through a program of Arms control treaty withdrawals and proliferation of missile defence initiatives aimed at neutralising Russia's nuclear strike capability. Other than Poseidon, the Russian counters include the Kinzhal air launched hypersonic missile, Burevestnik nuclear powered global range cruise missile and Avangard hypersonic exoatmospheric/atmospheric glide vehicle, all aimed at enhancing the nuclear deterrent forces of the Russian Federation.

Poseidon has two major operational roles. 1. Strike an adversaries naval bases and port facilities (this would essentially include coastal cities) with a special (nuclear) warhead in the event of a nuclear attack on the Russian Federation or one of her allies. 2. Strike NATO aircraft carrier/cruise missile carrier battle groups at sea with a nuclear warhead (in the event of nuclear strike on the Russian Federation or one of her allies) or conventional warhead in a conventional war scenario. The system is intended to travel oceanic distances at great depths and high speeds, defeating all current and projected near term NATO defense measures through a combination of high speed, stealth, guile and technological advances in self-protection capability. The latter would play an important part in ensuring the system remains viable as it approaches shallower water where its immunity from detection and attack systems would be reduced.

It has not been revealed which of the Russian submarine design houses and builders are involved in development of the Poseidon Oceanic Multipurpose System. In regards to design there are a number of candidate design houses, in particular CDB ME-Rubin and Malachite SPB. The latter bureau in particular has considerable experience in design work on a plethora of small size littoral submarines and submersibles. Another design bureau involved in deep sea submersible design is CDB-Lazurit. There are a number of candidates for construction of the Poseidon drones – Admiralty Shipyards and JSC Bars being among those builders currently (2019) involved in submersible building (Harkins, 2019).

There are few confirmed details available regarding the Poseidon Oceanic Multipurpose System. As best can be determined, from sparse details and available graphics released by the Russian Federation government, the system consists of three distinct undersea elements – the Poseidon UUV (Uninhabited Underwater Vehicle) deep ocean submersible, the warhead carrying vehicle, which appears to be a torpedo like craft that is apparently deployed from the UUV, and the mothership submarine.

MODRF (Ministry of Defence of the Russian Federation) graphics depicting the Poseidon UUV, which would incorporate the main propulsion system (small nuclear reactor) and a suite of sensors to allow it to autonomously navigate the oceans at great depths, show a more or less cylindrical vehicle (not completely as the side walls appear to be slightly flattened in appearance) tapering inwards toward the extreme rear section. Main control surfaces consist of four surfaces arrayed in a 'X' cruciform layout about midway down the taper at the rear of the vehicle. The propulsion propeller complex is arrayed in a cruciform layout aft of the control surfaces, the propellers themselves being extended on protruding shafts. It is not possible to determine from released data whether there are any thruster controls installed on the vehicle. There is a pronounced central hump atop the cylindrical body of the vehicle, this being reminiscent of a conning tower (sail) found on a typical submarine design, but with a different function on the UUV.

Page 4-5: Graphics depicting a Poseidon UUV housed in a launch cradle within the open internal carriage bay on a nuclear powered submarine (previous page top), being launched from the upper section of the nuclear powered submarine mothership (previous page bottom) and ascending from the mothership submarine (this page). Kremlin Press Service/MODRF

A graphic released by the MODRF in spring 2018 (top) show what appears to be a warhead vehicle element of the Poseidon Oceanic Multipurpose System. The layout appears to be similar to that of a torpedo, although scale-comparisons are not possible through released graphic and photographic material. The propulsion system appears to drive a propeller system in the graphic (top), but the photographic material released has been intentionally blurred out in this sensitive area (above).
MODRF

The warhead carrying vehicle appears reminiscent of a torpedo like craft, having a long cylindrical body, four large all-moving control surfaces arrayed in a cruciform layout toward the rear section. Aft of the control surfaces is the propulsion expeller section, which may be a propeller complex as found on a conventional torpedo, or, perhaps, an air-jet propulsion unit, the former, supported by graphic evidence, being the most likely. Photographic evidence, released by the MODRF, suggests that the warhead carrying vehicle would be housed in a launch tube structure. However, this is unconfirmed (March 2019) and the structure surrounding the vehicle may be a protective structure for storage. Although unconfirmed, TASS (Russian News Agency) reported, citing unnamed sources within the Russian defence industry, that the warhead element of the Poseidon complex would have a yield of 2 megatons, enabling it to destroy its primary targets – naval bases and ports. As of March 2019, warhead yield has not been confirmed the MODRF. Although the primary mission against ports and naval bases requires a nuclear warhead, the secondary mission, destruction of sea surface battle groups, may be carried out with a nuclear or conventional warhead. The warhead vehicle, which would be launched from the Poseidon UUV at an undetermined distance from the target, would incorporate an advanced sensor suite to allow it to navigate and home on the target in the terminal cruise phase – sea going or area costal target (naval base or port).

Released in 2019, this still of an element of the Poseidon system shows the torpedo like warhead vehicle housed in a protective canister. MODRF

While photographic images of what appears to be the warhead vehicle test-bed have been released, no photographic images of the Poseidon UUV have been released. This precludes any scale comparison of the two. This unknown presents problems in attempts to assess with, any degree of confidence, as to the area of the Poseidon UUV that the warhead vehicle would be carried within and deployed from, as well as the number of warhead vehicles carried. No data has been released on the number of warhead deployment vehicles to be carried – this may be a single warhead only as suggested by released graphic data showing only a single warhead vehicle.

The 200 km/h (~108 knots) speed specified, apparently proven during trials in 2019, for the Poseidon system would provide the capability to engage all current and projected large surface combatants (typically demonstrating speeds of ~30 knots) when employed in the anti-surface battle group mission. It should be noted that released data does not make clear, with absolute certainty, whether the quoted speed of 200 km/h applies to the Poseidon UUV or the deployed warhead vehicle. However, a 2 February 2019 statement at Russian Federation government level, to the effect that the key stage of trials that had been completed involved a period of sea trials that confirmed the unlimited trans-oceanic range and 200+ km/h speed, suggests that this speed value was relevant for the Poseidon UUV. If this is the case then it leaves open the question of the speed value for the warhead vehicle.

Previous page: Series of graphics depicting the nuclear powered multipurpose submarine Poseidon UUV carrier mothership. The graphics certainly appear reminiscent of a Project 949A derivative. Top: The only new design class of submarine other than the 949A derivatives that would be expected to have the volume to accommodate the Poseidon UUV is the Project 954A. Above: This still has been extracted from a MODRF release of the Poseidon concept. It depicts a nuclear submarine undergoing deep maintenance or modification – one being left to infer that it may be a conversion for the planned operational Poseidon mothership or, perhaps, a modification to a submarine for Poseidon sea trials. MODRF

Information regarding the mothership Poseidon UUV carrier submarines is conflicting. References to new build submarines have been made at Russian presidential level. Other sources (unnamed and therefore lacking authority) indicate conversions from the existing nuclear powered submarine fleet – operational and or non-operational. On 20 February 2019, the Russian President confirmed that the first Poseidon carrying mothership nuclear powered submarine would be launched in spring of that year (TASS). This statement was likely the fuel for firing up the early 2019 TASS report, quoting unnamed defence industry sources, that the Poseidon UUV were to be carried by new generation nuclear powered submarines then being built at PO Sevmash. The types of nuclear powered attack and ballistic missile submarines under construction or planned in Russia at the time of this announcement were of the Project 885M Yasen-M multipurpose nuclear submarine cruiser and Project 955A Borey-A underwater Strategic Missile Carrier types respectively. The available evidence suggests that the Project 955A submarines are being built exclusively as strategic missile carriers armed with Bulava SLBM (Submarine Launched Ballistic Missiles) (Harkins, 2018). In regard to the Project 885M submarines, it is unlikely that such vessels would have the capacity to carry the Poseidon UUV internally, even in the absence of basic characteristics of the Poseidon vehicle. However, it is clear that there has been a revival in production of the Project 885M – the Project 885M *Ulyanovsk* was laid down on 27 July 2017 (Malachite & PO Sevmash).

Page 10-11: These views of Project 949/A (NATO reporting name Oscar/II) nuclear powered submarines serve to illustrate the large size of the class, which is vastly increased in area and displacement in the Project 08952 and 08951 Project 949A derivatives. PO Sevmash

Contradicting the new generation submarine Poseidon carrier design hypothesis, there has been speculation, citing unnamed sources within the Russian defence industry, that the mothership submarines would be drawn from the existing Project 949A fleet of Submarine Missile Cruiser. A report emerged from the Russian state news agency that a pair of special derivatives of Project 949A Antey (NATO reporting name 'Oscar' II) were being built at Sevmash (TASS). There is no evidence to suggest a resumption of standard Project 949A building. However, it has been forwarded that the *Bolgorad* (an incomplete Project 949A initially laid down in 1992, but not completed due to the economic drawdown in Russia following the dissolution of the Soviet Union the previous year) was being further developed as the Project 09852 Special Purpose Submarine to accommodate research facilities for inhabited deep diving craft (this would now include the Poseidon UUV) and another special purpose submarine, the Project 09851, named *Khabarovsk*, was being prepared as a Poseidon carrier. The *Khabarovsk* is widely stated to have been laid down at Sevmash on 27 July 2014, along with the fifth Project 955A Borey-A class and a Project 885M Yasen class boat (TASS). However, PO Sevmash documentation confirms only the Project 885M and the Project 955A Borey-A class as having been laid down on this date (PO Sevmash). What little information that has been made available suggests (unconfirmed) that the *Khabarovsk* would be equipped for the carriage of deep diving submersibles and new weapon complexes – these may well be one in the same in the shape of Poseidon Oceanic Multipurpose System. In regards to the *Bolgorad*, TASS reports suggest that this is the submarine that the Russian presidential statement indicated would be launched in spring 2019. Further data indicates that this boat will be the first operational platform for the Poseidon UUV, six of which would be carried. To accommodate the Poseidon UUV, and potentially other deep diving submersibles, the *Bolgorad* has apparently been redesigned from its original planned configuration that was similar to the Project 949A. A hull extension has apparently been incorporated to house the Poseidon UUV's and their respective launch apparatus. This would significantly increase the length and displacement of the *Bolgorad* over that of the 144 m (length) and 12500/22500 tons (surface and submerged displacement respectively) of the Project 949A. Length is expected to stretch ~30 m longer than the 949A (unconfirmed). Claims that the *Bolgorad* will emerge as the largest submarine ever built cannot be substantiated in the absence of verifiable data, however, it is unlikely to exceed the 48000 tons submerged displacement of the Project 941. It would be prudent to expect that the Project 09851 *Khabarovsk* would emerge in a similar configuration to that of the *Bolgorad*. The Project 949A has surface and submerged speeds of 16 and 32 knots respectively and an operational immersion depth of 600 m (MODRF), it being prudent to expect the Projects 09852 and 09851 to emerge with similar operational values.

Previous page top: Starboard profile of a Project 949A Antey Submarine Missile Cruiser. Previous page bottom: The Project 949A Submarine Missile Cruiser *Oryol* following modernisation at STAR in 2017. Above: Satellite image of a Project 949A Submarine Missile Cruiser at Severodvinsk in Northern Russia in October 2018. This vessel was undergoing maintenance, refit or modernisation. PO Sevmash/STAR/Google Earth

It has to be considered that the four planned Poseidon carriers may not necessarily be of the same class – indeed the *Bolgorad* and *Khabarovsk* have different project numbers – 09852 and 09851 respectively. Russia has a number of extant former service submarines that could be converted to carry Poseidon – these include retired Project 667BDR/BDRM submarines and even the retired Project 941 Akula class, no less than three of which remained at Severodvinsk in 2018 with a fourth serving with the Northern Fleet in an operational/trials role It would also be possible to redesign some of the existing operational fleet of Project 949A cruise missile carrier submarines to operate as Poseidon carriers. In 2018 the MODRF announced that the Project 949A fleet would undergo an armament capability modernisation, which would include incorporation of the Kalibre ASM/LACM (Anti-Ship Missile/Land Attack Cruise Missile) as replacement for the P-700 Granit supersonic ASM/LACM. Such a capability could be carried over to the Poseidon motherships, although on a reduced scale as the number of cruise missiles to be carried would be considerably reduced.

In late December 2018, the MODRF confirmed that a nuclear powered submarine was employed as a Poseidon UUV carrier during sea trials (MODRF). The name, or class, of the submarine was not disclosed. It is equally unclear the manner in which the Poseidon vehicle was carried – internal or external. The former would have required considerable modifications to the mother ship.

The primary mission, as noted above, is the destruction of an aggressor's naval bases and or ports with a nuclear warhead in the event of a nuclear attack on the

Russian Federation or one of her allies. Assuming deployment against a CONUS (Continental United States) target, potential operational scenarios could involve the Poseidon UUV being employed in North Atlantic, North Pacific or Arctic ocean regions, this latter region, however, being relatively bereft of the type of primary target set the complex is intended to operate against.

Previous page: Series of stills showing the launch bay doors on the Poseidon mothership opening (top), the Poseidon UUV exits the launch bay (centre) and cruises past the coning tower of the mothership submarine following launch (bottom). This page: The warhead delivery vehicle cruises to the target at undetermined depths. The vehicle is depicted here cruising just above the ocean floor (top) and approaching the primary target for the Poseidon Oceanic Multi-Purpose System – an adversary's naval base (above). MODRF

The secondary mission, as noted above, is the destruction of enemy aircraft carrier/cruise missile carrier battle groups on the high seas, this being confirmed by the MODRF, 'Poseidon is 100% invulnerable to enemy countermeasures. The drones unique capabilities will enable the Russian Navy to fight carrier-led and surface action groups of potential enemy in areas of the oceanic theatre... operations and strike coastal infrastructure facilities at an intercontinental distance' (MODRF). This relative invulnerability comes courtesy of the extreme operating depths and high speed of the complex, both of which traits would provide NATO naval forces with difficulties of detection, and interception would prove ineffective by current and near term projected ASW (Anti-Submarine Warfare) defensive systems. The secondary target set – aircraft carrier and cruise missile carrier battle groups – are less likely to be encountered in the Arctic region than they are in the North Atlantic and North Pacific oceans and adjacent seas. When employed in the secondary anti-surface group role the Poseidon UUV can, as noted above, be armed with nuclear or conventional warheads. The TNT equivalent weight of the conventional warhead is an unknown as of March 2019.

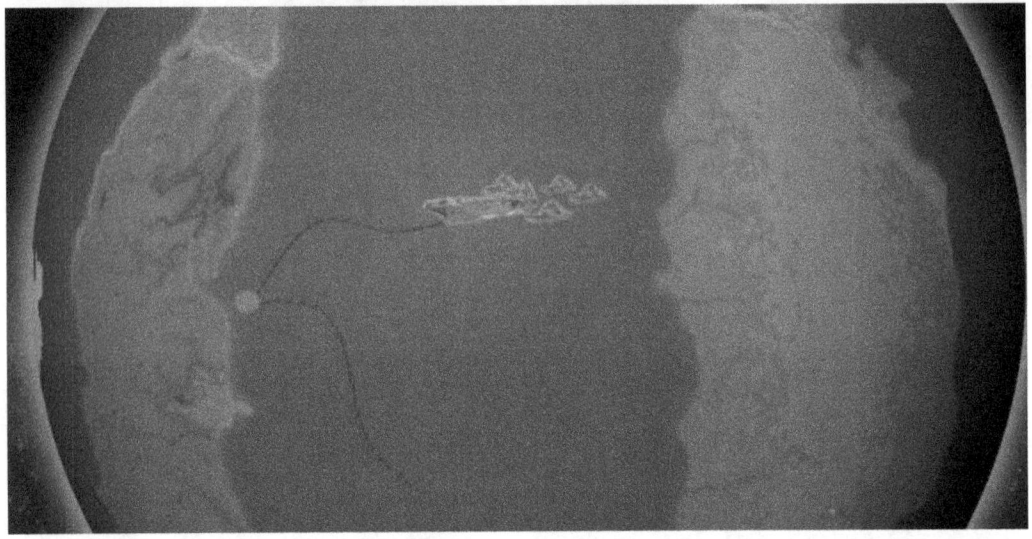

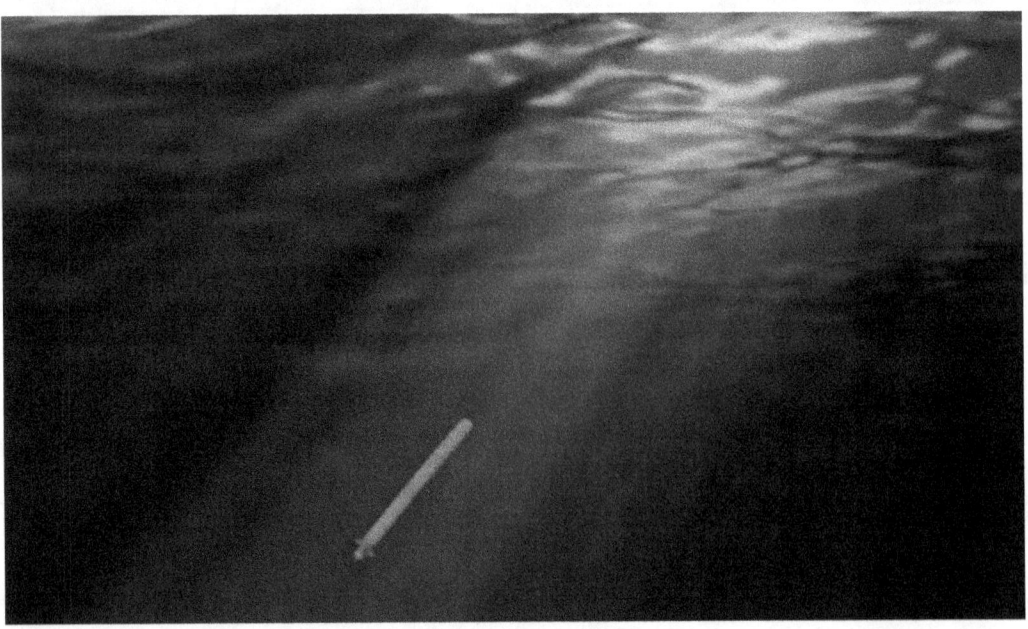

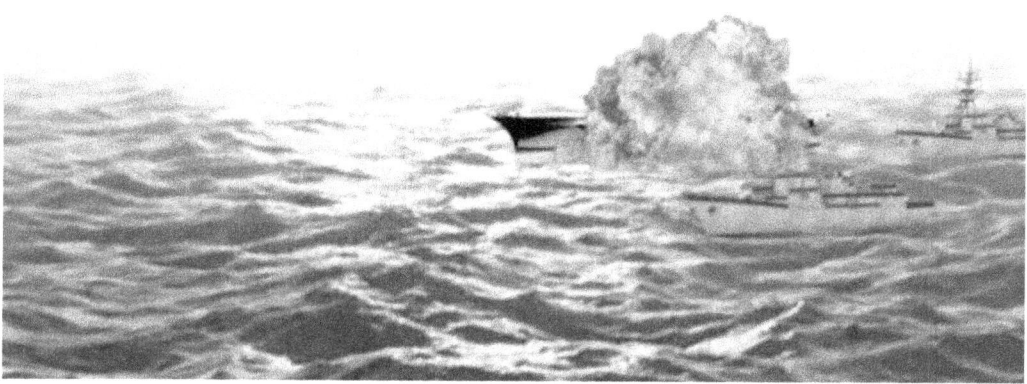

Page 16-17: This series of graphics depicts the Poseidon Oceanic Multipurpose System being employed in its secondary anti-surface group mission, armed with a conventional warhead. The mothership launches the Poseidon UUV (previous page top), the warhead delivery vehicle, following release from the Poseidon UUV and cruise to the target area, commences a high inclination attack profile against the surface warship (previous page bottom), the warship being destroyed by the warhead (above). MODRF

Although the conventional strike warhead would be of small-scale destructive power in comparison to a nuclear warhead, it would prudent to expect it to be sufficient to sink or disable a large warship such as an aircraft carrier or cruiser or a large merchant vessel such as a container ship or supertanker. The threat Poseidon would pose to naval bases and ports in a conventional conflict scenario could force a potential adversary to divert resources from offensive systems, able to be forward deployed, to defensive systems for home defence. In any case, the capability intended with introduction of the Poseidon Oceanic Multipurpose System would allow that complex to become an asymmetric counter to the enormous offensive power of NATO aircraft carrier/cruise missile carrier surface battle groups. An aircraft carrier battle group costing several tens of billions of dollars could be countered by Poseidon at a cost of perhaps several tens of millions of dollars.

It is unclear, in 2019, what the operational dispositions for Poseidon operations will be. Will the system be deployed on deterrent patrols in a similar manner to that carried out by ballistic missile armed submarines? Or would it be deployed operationally only in times of tension or conflict? In either case, on a primary mission launch distance of 500 km from an enemy shore, this would reduce to around 2.5 hours the time required to strike a fixed coastal target from the point of launch to target destruction. This would be considerably less than the 24 hours plus that may be required to strike an oceanic range target from Russian littoral regions. It can be assumed that the oceanic range would allow for Poseidon's launch from a shore base against strategic targets. However, such a scenario would, as would be the case for launch from a submarine in Russian littoral waters, entail an oceanic voyage perhaps exceeding 24 hours when operating against a CONUS target.

It may be possible for the submarine motherships to replenish while at sea, extending time on station during non-war operations or replenishing warheads in wartime. This latter operation would of course put the vessel at high risk unless it was conducted in sea areas controlled by Russia. PO Sevmash

A weapon in the class of Poseidon has many disadvantages compared with traditional nuclear delivery platforms such as ballistic/aero-ballistic or cruise missiles, not least of which is the speed of warhead delivery to a target. The 200 km/h speed of Poseidon would be relatively pedestrian compared to the hypersonic speeds of modern delivery systems in the mold of the Avangard hypersonic glide vehicle. For the anti-surface group mission, a major advantage that the deployment of Poseidon would have over missiles, even those with hypersonic speeds, would be increased survivability of the launch platform. Launching missiles, hypersonic (for naval operations this would be the Tsirkon), supersonic or subsonic, requires the launch platform to come up to a depth of less than 100 m – ~50 m being considered standard. This would bring the submarine into the effective operating environment of defensive countermeasures, which may prevent missile launch at a crucial time or place the launch platform in jeopardy just prior to, during, or following the launch phase. Poseidon would overcome this problem as the UUV would be released at depths exceeding the capability of countermeasures. Poseidon could also be employed against targets beyond the relative safe operating reach of aircraft/missile combinations or submarine launched hypersonic cruise missiles.

One operational area that there has been no information release on is that of the reuse or disposability of the Poseidon UUV – is it a one shot deal or is the Poseidon UUV recovered by the mothership submarine following launch of the warhead vehicle? Assuming the latter, then, following the UUV rendezvous with the mothership submarine at predetermined coordinates, recovery by the mothership submarine would be conducted along similar lines to that of recovery of inhabited submersibles carried by submarines for other purposes. The recovery process would be fully automated and controlled from the mothership.

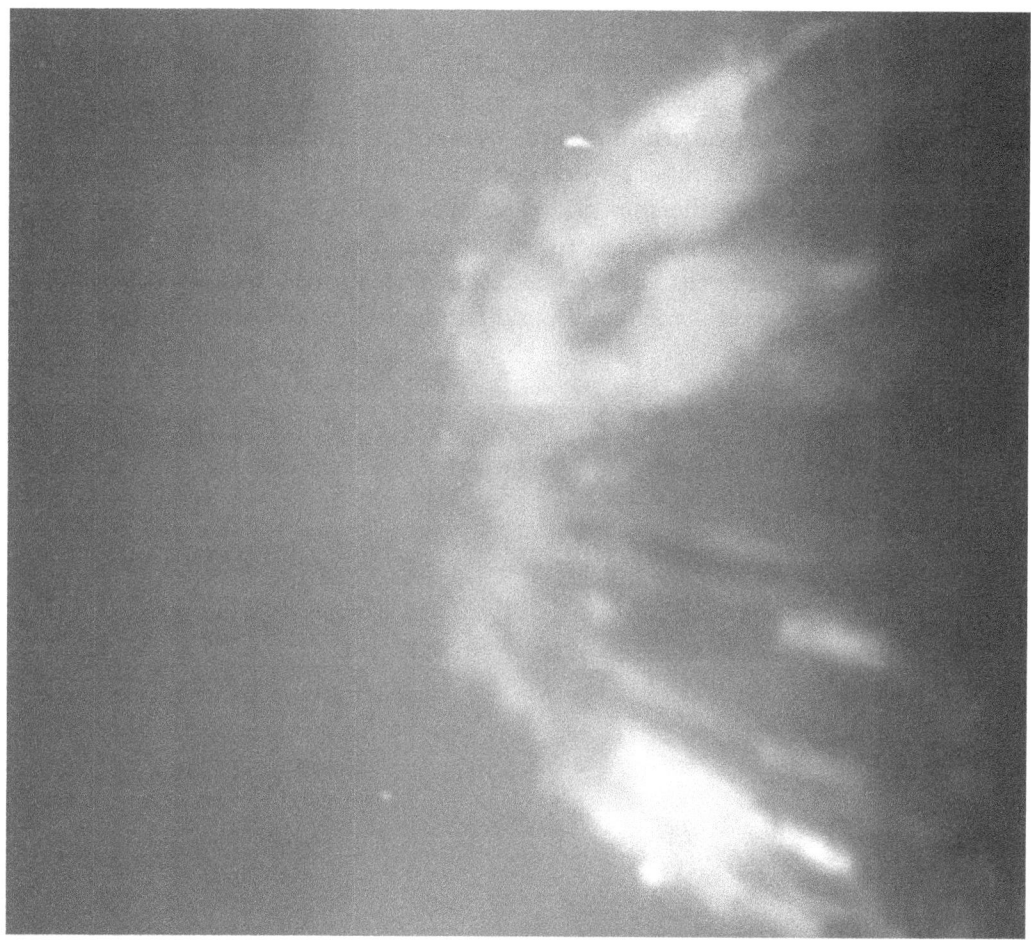

On 19 July 2018, the MODRF confirmed that the Poseidon UUV complex trials had commenced. The statement continued:

> "Trials have been organized at the ranges of the Defence Ministry of Russia to confirm the dynamic characteristics of the apparatus during launches in a real environment and to check the parameters of the apparatus's movement along the route in autonomous mode" (MODRF).

Further elaboration by the MODRF in July 2018 confirmed that trials programs for various elements of the Poseidon Oceanic Multipurpose System were coming to an end and that the systems invulnerability to a potential adversaries countermeasures had been proven. Such invulnerability would be achieved through a combination of operational traits – cruise immersion depth considerably below the effective parameters of current or planned ASW systems, a very high operating underwater speed and unpredictable mission profiles for approaching the target.

Another key stage of Poseidon trials was completed on 2 February 2019. This phase, which involved a period of sea trials, apparently confirmed, as noted above, the unlimited trans-oceanic range and 200+ km/h operating speed of the complex. For this phase of trials, the Poseidon vehicle had installed an operational reactor – the viability of the small nuclear reactor for the Poseidon UUV power plant had been proven through a series of development and trials programs, which had been completed in December 2017 (MODRF). The February 2019 trials were not in themselves full-scale sea trials for Poseidon, but rather an element of the overall experimental work being carried out on the overall Poseidon system.

Whilst Poseidon development work continued in the first quarter of 2019, the Project 09852 *Belgorod* mothership dockyard trials were scheduled to be conducted through 2019 and the boat was expected to be commissioned into the Russian Navy – most likely the Northern Fleet – in 2020. The Project 09851 *Khabarovsk*, is scheduled to be launched sometime around spring 2020 and assume an operational capability in 2022.

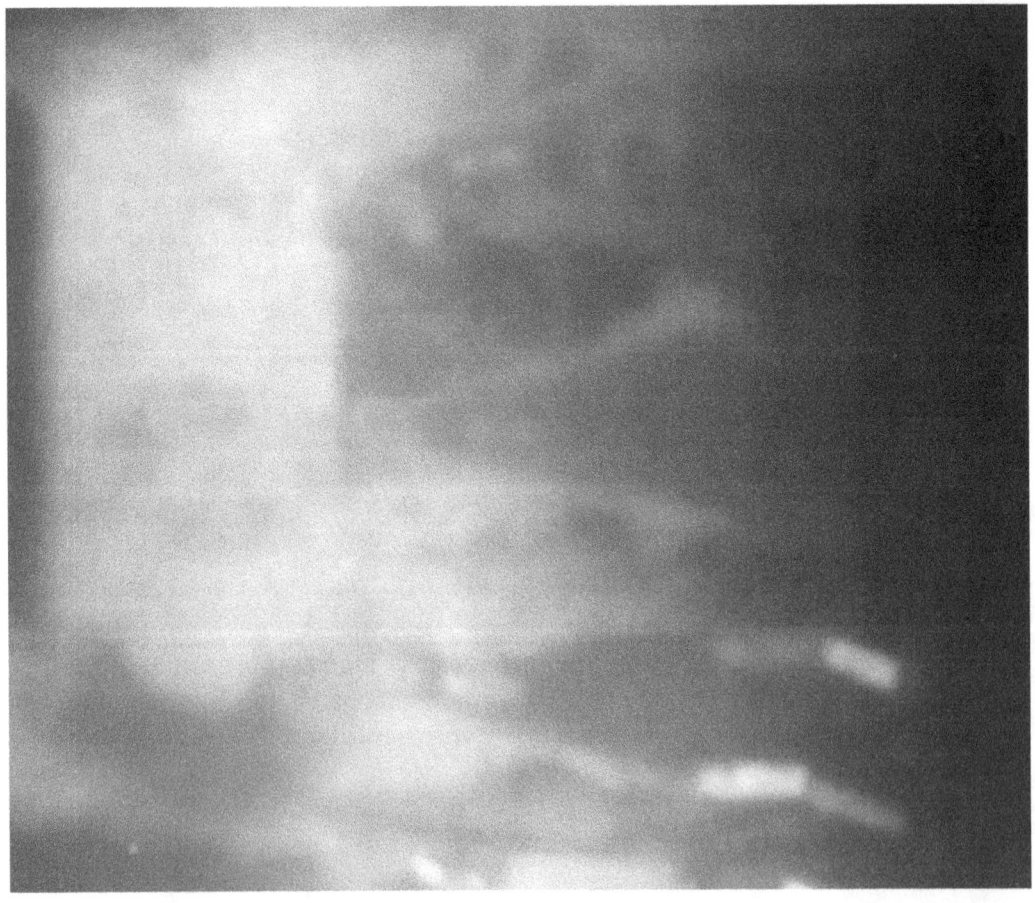

Page 19-20: Stills showing a launch phase during the sea trials conducted in early 2019. This appears to be the launch of the warhead vehicle from the Poseidon UUV, although this has not been confirmed by the **MODRF.** MODRF

Although unconfirmed by the MODRF or at Russian Federation government level, TASS reported that the Poseidon program would be procured within the 2018-2027 state armament plan. Current planning appears to call for four Poseidon carrier submarines – two for the Northern Fleet and two for the Pacific Fleet (these are the fleets currently operating the Russian ballistic missile submarines) – to be commissioned, each armed with six Poseidon UUV. This appears to equate to a requirement for 24 operational Poseidon drones (unconfirmed). Other estimates put the requirement at 32 Poseidon UUV and the number to be carried by each carrier submarine at eight. It is unlikely that there would be a requirement for a full complement of Poseidon UUV for all four submarine carriers as at least one would be expected to be undergoing maintenance or refit at all times, and thus be deemed non-operational. Additional vehicles would be required for training and trials.

The only graphic material on the mothership employed on the early 2019 sea trials is this image of waves crashing on the unidentified nuclear submarine. MODRF

While there are detractors from the school of thought, the available evidence and projected capability levels suggest that the Poseidon Oceanic Multipurpose System would provide the Russian Federation with an additional viable nuclear strike capability that is immune to current ASW defence systems. Other measures to overcome NATO missile defence systems include the introduction of hypersonic missiles, such as Kinzhal (Mach 10) and the Tsirkon (this Mach 8 missile, intended for submarine or surface ship launch, is still in development in 2019), the new generation SARMAT ICBM (Intercontinental Ballistic Missile) with increased penetration capabilities and the Avangard hypersonic glide vehicle carried on the missile phase of the trajectory by an ICBM, the glide vehicle then reentering the dense layers of atmosphere and maneuvering to its target at high hypersonic speed – ~Mach 20.

The effective demise of the INF (Intermediate range Nuclear Forces) treaty (suspended by the United States in February 2019 and, in response, by Russia in March 2019) leaves only the New START (Strategic Arms Reduction Treaty) to limit nuclear warheads and their delivery systems. Russia has expressed concern at NATO rebuffs to its attempts to enter into talks aimed at extending New START, (this treaty is due expire in February 2021) this uncertainty being added to by NATO nations refusal to ratify an extension to the nuclear test ban treaty. Development and introduction of new advanced weapon systems, able to counter NATO attempts to nullify Russia's strategic nuclear deterrent forces as the alliance pushes for global hegemony, may be seen as a two pronged spear. If the US opts to let New START expire then the new Russian strategic weapon systems will ensure Russia's security against what it perceives as an aggressive NATO alliance with territorial ambitions against the Russian Federation and her allies, even in a climate of increased strategic weapon deployment by NATO. On the other hand, weapon systems such as the Poseidon Oceanic Multipurpose System, provide the Russian Federation with the strategic strike currency it requires to convince NATO to accept the late Cold War principle that neither side can win a nuclear war. While the dream of multilateral nuclear disarmament is just that, a dream, it has to be hoped that decision makers will embrace the pragmatism of their forebears of the 1970's and 1980's and push toward a policy of arms control agreements and nuclear parity – embrace the pragmatic view that neither side can win a full-scale nuclear war against the other.

In regards to the employment of Poseidon in a nuclear role it is pertinent to look at the nuclear posture of the Russian Federation and NATO. While NATO circulates contradictory documentation stating that whilst Russia lowers the threshold for nuclear weapons use the NATO alliance does not follow this path, a study of the nuclear postures of both sides provides clear evidence that the contrary is actually true. The current Russian Federation nuclear posture envisages one of two thresholds would have to be crossed before a nuclear strike can be authorised: 1. When Russia or one of her allies has been attacked with nuclear weapons. 2. When the very existence of the Russian Federation as a sovereign nation is threatened. By contrast, the NATO alliance is fostering plans to move forward with a doctrine that lower the threshold for a nuclear strike on an adversary. The February 2018 NPR (Nuclear Posture Review) appears to suggest that the US would employ nuclear weapons against an adversary that had employed conventional weapons against the US or one of her allies. Furthermore, the 2018 NPR places greater emphasis on the use of nuclear weapons compared to the 2010 NPR. The 2018 NPR goes further by embracing the concept of limited nuclear exchanges, a posture pondered and abandoned as unsound during the high threat days of the late Cold War era.

The advocating by the US of the use of nuclear weapons in a conflict that has, until that point, been waged with conventional weapons, may have a bearing on the composition of Poseidon aboard the mothership submarine – a mix of nuclear and conventional warheads for a carrier submarine on patrol rather than all nuclear as it could not be ruled out that NATO could launch a nuclear strike during an otherwise conventional conflict whilst the Poseidon UUV carrier is at sea. Of course, the lack of available information regarding Poseidon in 2019 means it cannot be ruled out that a change can be made from nuclear to conventional warheads onboard the mothership submarine.

The Poseidon Oceanic Multipurpose System is one of a number of new technology developments pursued by the Russian Federation to counter what, as noted above, that nation perceives as NATO ongoing attempts to neutralise Russia's nuclear strike capability through a number of means, including withdrawal from arms control treaties – the ABM (Anti-Ballistic Missile) in 2002 and the INF (suspended in 2019). Withdrawal from the former facilitated NATO plans, later actioned, to circle (not literally) the Russian Federation with missile defence systems while withdrawal from the latter is considered by Russia as a first step in the deployment of INF range class missiles close to Russia's borders (no information exists to suggest this would be case, but it remains a possibility). This would vastly increase NATO's first strike capability and the scope for nuclear escalation of a conflict, considering that the Russia Federation would have to respond by installing INF range class missiles in her European regions. While the threat of a nuclear exchange between NATO and the Soviet Union (later the Russian Federation) reduced, considerably in the late 1980's and more or less fell into obscurity in the 1990's, the demise of the ABM, suspension of INF and the threat to an extension to New START, has placed nuclear weapons and their delivery systems back to the fore toward the end of the second decade of the twenty first century.

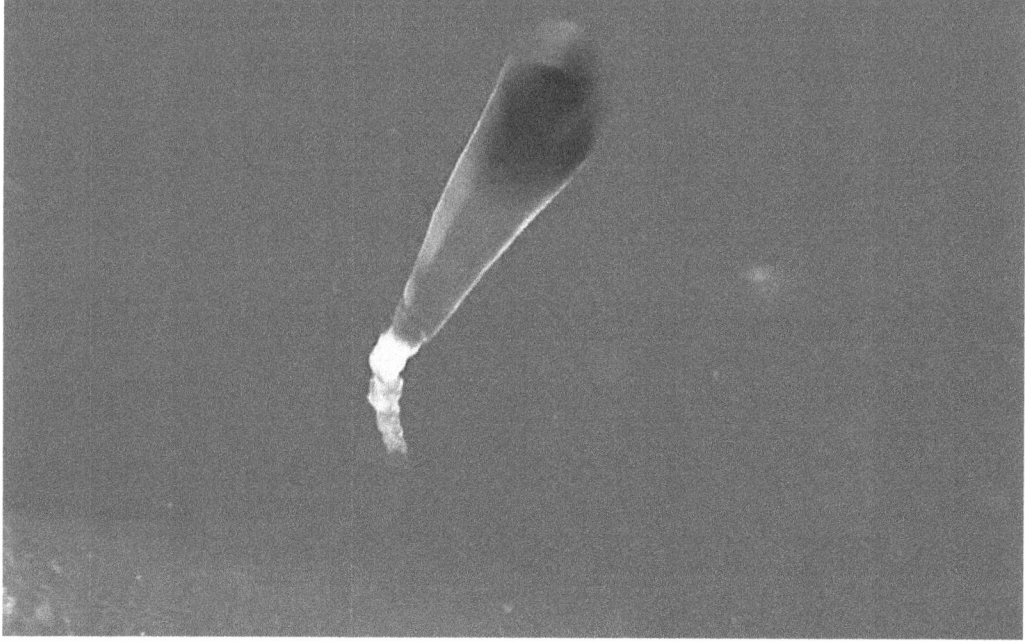

This graphic appears to depict the Poseidon Oceanic Multipurpose System warhead delivery vehicle travelling at high underwater speed. MODRF

GLOSSARY

ABM	Anti-Ballistic Missile
ASM	Anti-Ship Missile
ASW	Anti-Submarine Warfare
CDB	Central Design Bureau
CONUS	Continental United States
ICBM	Intercontinental Ballistic Missile
INF	Intermediate range Nuclear Forces – 500-5500 km missiles
JSC	Joint Stock Company
Km/h	Kilometers per hour
LACM	Land Attack Cruise Missile
Megatons	1 Megaton = 1,000.000 tons of TNT
MODRF	Ministry of Defence of the Russian Federation
NATO	North Atlantic Treaty Organisation
NPR	Nuclear Posture Review
SLBM	Submarine Launched Ballistic Missiles
START	Strategic Arms Reduction Treaty
TNT	Trinitrotoluene – a high explosive chemical formation
US	United States
UUV	Uninhabited Underwater Vehicle
~	Approximately equal to (can also be used to mean asymptotically equal)

ABOUT THE AUTHOR

Hugh Harkins FRAS is a historian and author with an extensive research background in astro/geophysics and studies/research in the wider scientific, aeronautic, astronautic and nautical technical and historical fields. He is also involved in research in the field of Scottish history, which formed a significant element of an otherwise scientific undergraduate degree. Hugh has published in excess of sixty books; non-fiction and fiction, writing under his given name as well as utilising several pseudonyms. He has also written for several international magazines, whilst his work has been used as reference for many other projects, ranging from the aviation industry, international news corporations and film media to encyclopaedias, museum exhibits and the computer gaming industry. Hugh is a member of the Institute of Physics and is an elected Fellow of the Royal Astronomical Society. He currently resides in his native Scotland. Other titles by the author include:

Russian Littoral Submarines & Submersibles – Piranha/Piranha-T/P-550/P-650E/Triton-I/II/Rus & Bester
Russia's Coastal Missile Shield - Bal-E & Bastion Mobile Coastal Cruise Missile Complexes
Iskander - Mobile Tactical Aero-Ballistic/Cruise Missile Complex
Orbital/Fractional Orbit Bombardment System - The Soviet Globalnaya Raketa
Counter-Space Defence Co-Orbital Satellite Fighter
Russia's Strategic Missile Carrier/Bomber Roadmap 2018-2040 – PAK DA, Tu-160M2, Tu-95MSM & Tu-22M3M
Sukhoi T-50/PAK FA - Russia's 5th Generation 'Stealth' Fighter
Sukhoi Su-35S 'Flanker' E - Russia's 4++ Generation Super-Manoeuvrability Fighter
Sukhoi Su-34 'Fullback'
Sukhoi Su-30MKK/MK2/M2 - Russo Kitashiy Striker from Amur
Soviet Mixed Power Experimental Fighter Aircraft – Piston-Liquid Propellant Rocket Engine/Piston-Ramjet/Piston-Pulsejet & Piston-Compressor Jet Engine Designs of the 1940's
MiG-35/D 'Fulcrum' F – Towards the Fifth Generation
Air War over Syria, Tu-160, Tu-95MS & Tu-22M3 - Cruise Missile and Bombing Strikes on Syria, November 2015-February 2016
Sukhoi Su-27SM(3)/SKM
Russian/Soviet Aircraft Carrier & Carrier Aviation Design & Evolution Volume 1 - Seaplane Carriers, Project 71/72, Graf Zeppelin, Project 1123 ASW Cruiser & Project 1143-1143.4 Heavy Aircraft Carrying Cruiser
Light Battle Cruisers and the Second Battle of Heligoland Bight
British Battlecruisers of World War 1 - Operational Log, July 1914-June 1915
Eurofighter Typhoon - Storm over Europe
North American F-108 Rapier - Mach 3 Interceptor
Convair YB-60 - Fort Worth Overcast
Boeing X-36 Tailless Agility Flight Research Aircraft
X-32 - The Boeing Joint Strike Fighter
X-35 - Progenitor to the F-35 Lightning II
X-45 Uninhabited Combat Air Vehicle
Into The Cauldron - The Lancaster MK.I Daylight Raid on Augsburg
Hurricane IIB Combat Log - 151 Wing RAF, North Russia 1941
RAF Meteor Jet Fighters in World War II, an Operational Log
Typhoon IA/B Combat Log - Operation Jubilee, August 1942
Defiant MK.I Combat Log - Fighter Command, May-September 1940
Blenheim MK.IF Combat Log - Fighter Command Day Fighter Sweeps/Night Interceptions, September 1939 - June 1940